I am
BLIND

I am BLIND

Brenda Pettenuzzo
meets
Nigel Weekes

Photography: Chris Fairclough

Consultants: RNIB

01024

FRANKLIN WATTS

London/New York/Sydney/Toronto

Nigel Weekes is nine years old. He is a registered blind person. He lives with his mum, Venice, and his sister, Shivaun, aged two, at home in Luton. During school time he stays from Monday to Friday at Linden Lodge, a school for children with visual impairment, in south London.

Contents

© 1988 Franklin Watts
12a Golden Square
LONDON W1

ISBN: 0 86313 698 2

Series Consultant: Beverley Mathias
Editor: Jenny Wood
Design: Edward Kinsey

Typesetting: Keyspools Ltd

Printed in Great Britain

The Publishers, Photographer and author would like to thank Nigel Weekes and his family for their great help and co- operation in the preparation of this book. Thanks are also due to Linden Lodge School and the RNIB for their help and advice.

Brenda Pettenuzzo is a Science and Religious Education teacher at St Angela's Ursuline Convent School, a Comprehensive School in the London Borough of Newham.

The first signs

"When I was born, there was nothing wrong with my sight as far as anyone could tell."

Nigel was a normal baby in every way. His mum took him for routine check-ups at the local clinic and he seemed to be developing in the usual way. As he grew older he went to mother and toddler groups and to playgroup. When he was about three-and-a-half years old people began to suspect that he was not seeing normally. His mum took him to the doctor.

"I go to the Eye Hospital every few months for a check-up."

The family doctor referred Nigel to the local hospital. The doctor there soon sent him to Moorfields Eye Hospital in London. The specialist found that one eye had become damaged. A part of the eye called the retina was coming away. Soon afterwards Nigel's other eye began to fail. The doctors do not know why this happened. Nigel's eyes have been getting steadily worse since then. Now he can see very little, especially when it is dark.

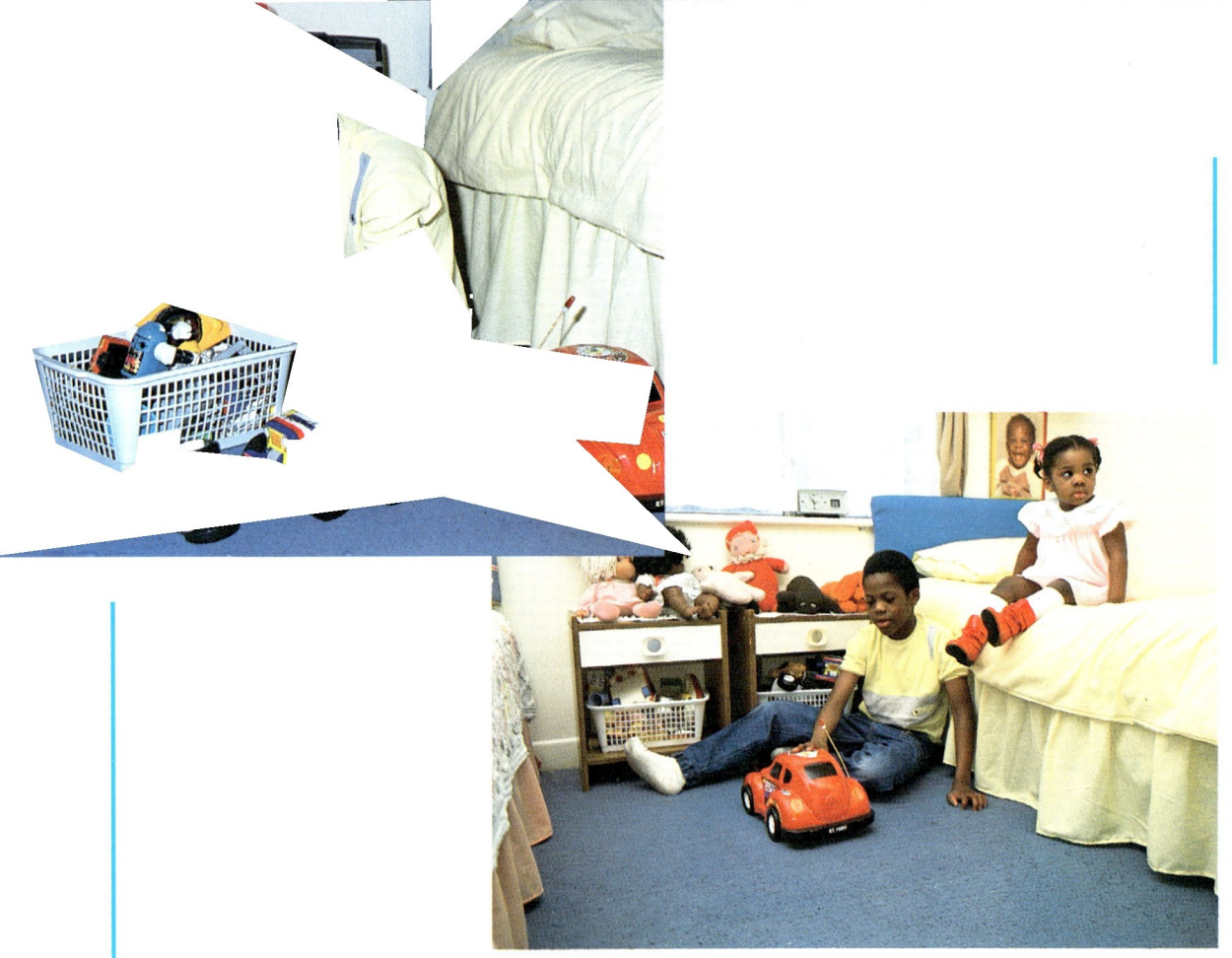

Playing at home

"When I'm at home I like to play in my bedroom. Sometimes I play with Shivaun but she doesn't always like my toys!"

Although Nigel's eyesight has grown worse over the years, he can play with many of his toys, such as the small cars, because he knows their shape very well. Sometimes he has to hold things very close to his eyes in order to look at them. The toys he likes best are those which are brightly coloured and interesting to feel.

8

"When I'm at home I often play with friends who live nearby. Sometimes we go out on our roller skates!"

Nigel's mum makes sure that he doesn't skate in a dangerous place. There is a playground near their home. Nigel can get there without having to cross a road. As well as skating, Nigel often plays on the swings at the playground. People who see Nigel skating and running find it hard to believe that he is almost blind. He moves about confidently because he knows where he is.

"I like to play 'Connect 4' with my mum. Sometimes I win, but usually Shivaun stops the game first!"

There are lots of games which Nigel can play. "Connect 4" is a good one because Nigel can see the different colours if the light is bright enough. There are many board games available now which have been adapted for people with poor eyesight. Some games are marked in braille so that sighted and non-sighted people can play together.

Helping at home

"My mum lets me help out at home. I like grating carrots when we have salad."

Many of the things which sighted people find easy can be difficult or dangerous for Nigel. He has worked out ways of doing things such as grating carrots which are safer for him. Now he can use the grater without grating his fingers. He learns many of these things at school, and, at home, he uses what he has learned.

Learning braille

"I've been at this school since last year. My teacher is called Adam and he's teaching me how to read and write braille."

The braille system is one which many blind and partially sighted people use. Each letter, and sometimes whole words or parts of words, is represented by a "cell" which has up to six raised dots in it. The reader feels these dots in order to "read" the letters or words. Nigel is lucky: his fingers are sensitive and he has begun to learn braille very quickly. He can use a special machine called a Perkins brailler to write braille on heavy paper.

A	J	S
B	K	T
C	L	U
D	M	V
E	N	X
F	O	Y
G	P	Z
H	Q	
I	R	W

"I sometimes use the braille 'n print machine at school."

Modern technology has meant the development of many new devices to help disabled people. This machine uses a computer printer. It translates what Nigel brailles into normal print. The print can be any size required. The school also has a closed-circuit TV system which can enlarge small print and display it on a TV screen. Many other devices, such as talking computers, are available.

Life at school

"We often do maths in class. I can use a calculator which talks to me!"

Sighted people take many things for granted –
calculators, scales and rulers, for example. Nigel has
learned how to use these and many other things at
school. He has been taught how to feel the
measurements on a ruler which has raised instead of
printed marks on it. His talking calculator tells him
which numbers he has pressed, and the answer.

"Once a week my class does cooking in the flat."

Learning how to cope with many aspects of everyday life is an important part of Nigel's education. One part of the school is set out as a flat, and pupils learn many things about looking after themselves. The kitchen is just like that of many homes, with one or two extras. The cupboards have their contents written on the doors in print and in braille. Nigel and his classmates gain confidence in handling everyday objects. They also learn how to use some of the useful gadgets which have been invented for people with poor sight.

"I like all kinds of music, and dancing. I'm learning to tap-dance at school."

Nigel has the opportunity to try out lots of musical instruments at school. He enjoys both listening to music and making music. Once a week a dance teacher visits his school. Nigel and his friends have been learning the basic steps of tap-dancing. Their teacher says they are quite good!

"We have a swimming pool at my school. I go swimming every week, and I've got a certificate on my bedroom wall at home."

Nigel likes swimming and he is good at it. Before his eyesight started to fail, he had been swimming with his mother. He knows what the swimming pool looks like. He has friends who have never been able to see. They can swim like Nigel, but unlike him they only know about the feel of the pool and the water. Swimming is an activity which can be very exciting for them.

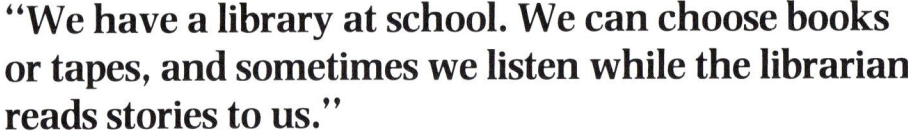

"We have a library at school. We can choose books or tapes, and sometimes we listen while the librarian reads stories to us."

The library at Linden Lodge has many books transcribed into braille. Some are very big: braille takes up more space than print, and the paper is usually thicker. Some of the books have braille *and* print in them. Each book has its title in braille on the cover, so that the pupils can read it. For those who prefer to listen, or who haven't yet learnt enough braille, there are tapes to be borrowed.

"No one goes home for dinner at my school. We have our lunch there and our breakfast and tea as well!"

Nigel's school is his home from Monday to Friday, so it's fortunate that he quite likes the school meals. Nigel sits with his friends at lunch, and there is usually a houseparent or a teacher at each table. Sometimes he can eat everything with no difficulty. Sometimes he needs a little help.

"Once a week I have a lesson with Julie, the Mobility Officer."

Every pupil spends some time with the Mobility Officer. She teaches them safe ways of finding their way around. Nigel's sight is much worse when the light is poor, but now he can find his way from his bedroom to the bathroom in the middle of the night! He moves around confidently at school and very rarely bumps into things.

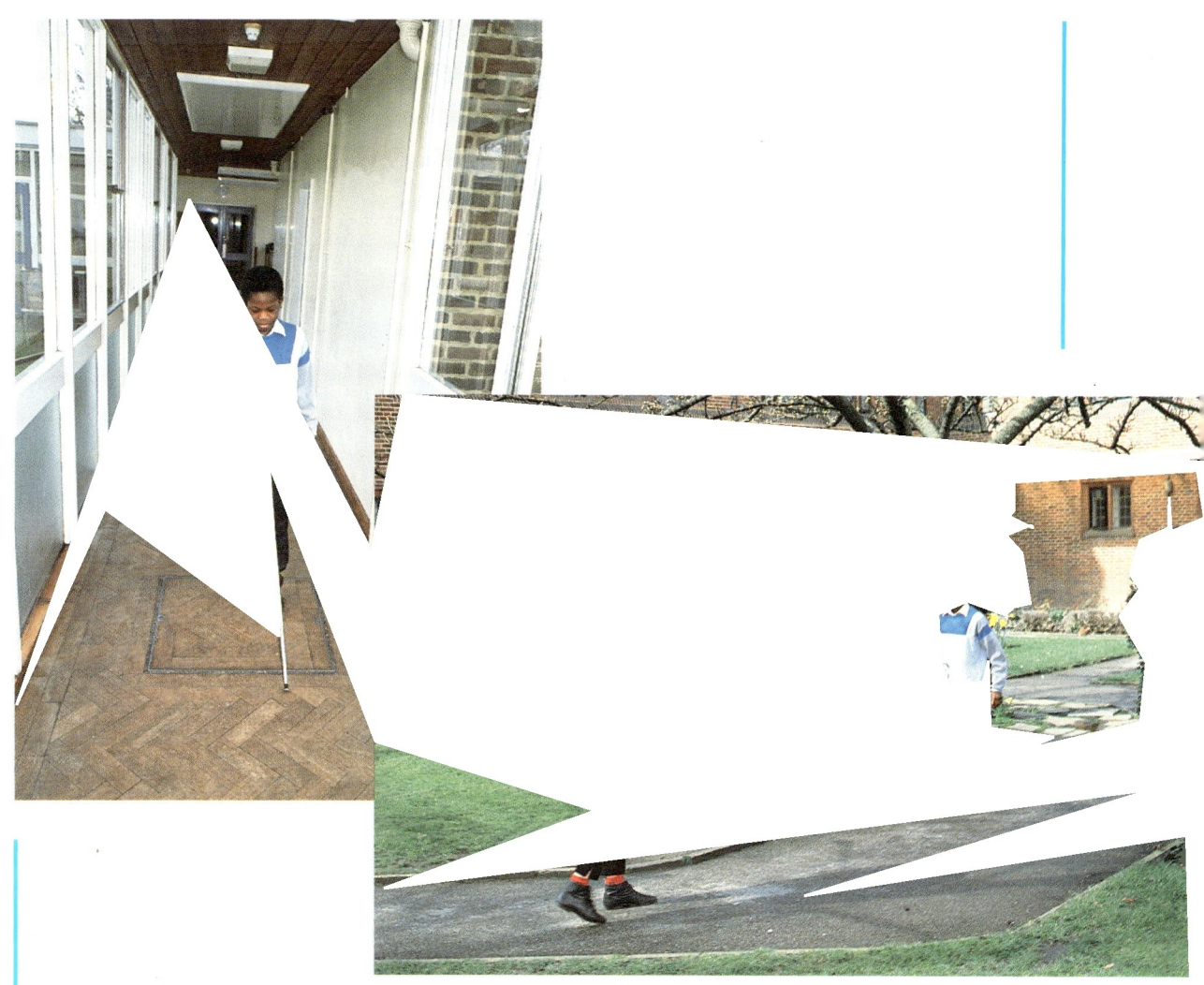

"Julie is teaching me how to use a cane. We sometimes go outside the school."

The aim of Nigel's mobility training is to make him able to get around on his own when he leaves school. Many of the pupils at his school are studying for exams and will go on to get all sorts of jobs. Mobility training will help them to be more independent when they leave school.

"I share my bedroom with Mark. Our names are on the door in print and braille. I can still read mine in print."

Nigel and Mark have brought things from home for their room and they like to keep it tidy. Keeping things in the right place is more important for people who cannot see well. It is easier for them to find something if it is where they expect it to be. There is a houseparent to help look after them, but being away from home has probably helped Nigel and his friends to be more independent. They have learnt to do many things for themselves.

"I do lots of things in my spare time at school. There is always someone to play with!"

Nigel can play with many of the toys and games which sighted people use. Building bricks are usually brightly coloured and easy to see. Nigel likes the feel of them as well. He enjoys a game of football just like many other boys and girls. Many blind people play with balls which make a noise so they can hear where the ball is.

"Since coming to Linden Lodge I've been a member of the Cub Scouts."

Nigel and many of the boys at his school belong to the local Cub Scout pack. This has other boys in it who live locally and are sighted. The Scout movement has always encouraged young people to join, regardless of what disability they have. As long as they understand the Scout promise they can be valuable members of the Scout movement.

On holiday

"Sometimes I go away with my mum and sister in the summer. This year I had a winter holiday with my school."

Nigel and some of his fellow pupils went skiing in Austria. They were very excited beforehand. It was Nigel's first time in an aeroplane, and he had no idea what skiing would feel like. Nowadays many blind and partially sighted people take part in all sorts of sports. There are blind climbers, horseriders and athletes of many kinds.

With the family

"Although I like my school, I look forward to being at home with my mum and my sister."

Nigel's little sister is too young to understand that there is anything wrong with his sight. To her he is just a hero! Nigel will always be a valued and loved member of his own family. With the help and support he gets at home and in school he should be able to take his place as a valued member of society as well. Blind people go into many different walks of life: politics, teaching, law, commerce, social work and many aspects of medicine. The list is endless!

Facts about blindness

When people talk about someone being "blind" they rarely mean a person who has no sight whatsoever. Many blind people have at least a sense of light and dark, if not some other perception, however short it falls of normal sight. There are about 42 million people in the world suffering from visual impairment, and even more with a less serious degree of handicap.

Several stages are involved in seeing:

1 Light passes into the eye through the transparent outer layer, or *cornea*.

2 The *lens* in the eye focuses the light on to the *retina*.

3 The retina receives the "picture" and transmits it along the *optic nerve* to the visual centre of the brain.

Most cases of impaired sight are due to one of these important parts of the eye being damaged. For some people, the damage is present from birth; for others, it is caused by illness or injury later on. Sometimes it is possible to repair the damage and restore some degree of sight. For example, if the cornea is damaged by chemical burns or scarring after infection, it may be possible to give the patient a new cornea by transplanting a healthy cornea

The Eye

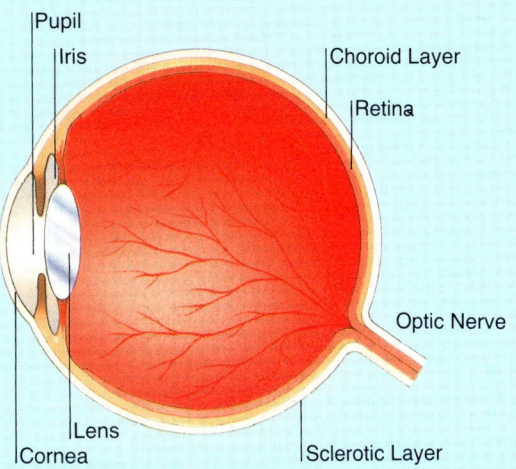

Pupil
Iris
Choroid Layer
Retina
Optic Nerve
Lens
Cornea
Sclerotic Layer

from the eye of someone who has just died and who wished certain of their organs to be used after their death to help other people.

Sometimes sight loss is due to the lens becoming opaque. This can be caused by certain diseases as well as by old age or radiation. If the lens is opaque, no light can pass through it and be focussed on to the retina. The retina, therefore, receives no "picture" to seen to the brain. Fortunately, it is possible to remove the lens and restore the sight, either by inserting a plastic replacement lens or by giving the person contact lenses or spectacles.

The most serious causes of blindness are those due to a failure of the retina. Injury can sometimes cause the retina to become detached from the back of the eye. Sometimes it is possible to re-attach parts of a retina and thus restore sight. There are several disorders which can affect the retina. Some are inherited conditions, while others are the effects of diseases. Sometimes they are caused by diseases of the blood system.

Some cases of blindness are caused by poisoning or side-effects from various drugs. And in the past, people have lost their sight as a result of mechanical injury to the eye. If an eye is penetrated by a dirty object, apart from the physical injury which results, an infection may also set in. Before the development of antibiotics this nearly always meant the loss of the eye, and frequently the sight in the other eye would soon be lost too. Now most infections can be treated with antibiotics and in many cases the sight is saved.

Every year in England and Wales about 200 children (under the age of fifteen) are added to the register of blind people. In the USA the number is four times as great. The most common cause of blindness in the young is a fault in the development of the eye itself or some part of it. Sometimes a fault is present and visible at birth, sometimes it does not become apparent until a number of years later. Many of the defects found in the eyes of young people are inherited from their parents, but some are caused by virus infections and other harmful agents passed from the mother through the placenta before birth. Some conditions result in the formation of cataracts (cloudiness of the lens), others cause the retina to degenerate rapidly.

There is a vast difference in the experience of blindness between those who are born blind and those who become blind later. The age at which blindness occurs also has a bearing on the way in which a person is able to cope with their disability. A child may be more able to accept and adapt to a situation than an adult who feels that their working life is finished because of their loss of sight. Someone who has always been blind may have no such adjustment problems, but will never have the advantage of the visual memory of the once sighted person. In the UK there are agencies which assist visually impaired people to lead lives which are as full and as normal as possible. These agencies may be funded by local or national government or by the National Health Service, or they may be voluntary organisations such as the Royal National Institute for the Blind (RNIB). Each local authority in the country keeps a register of blind people and a register of partially sighted people within its area of responsibility. Once someone has been placed on the appropriate register (usually on the recommendation of an eye specialist) the local authority, through its Social Services department, has a responsibility to make available various services for that person. The first step is usually to assign a social worker to the person, to assess the person's situation and try to work out their basic needs. A Technical Officer may be assigned to the person to help them overcome the various difficulties which blindness presents. A Mobility Officer may also be assigned, to assist the blind person in acquiring mobility skills which will broaden their horizons and make it easier for them to find employment if this is appropriate. Many of these services are available to blind children through their schools (special schools and mainstream schools).

Many children with a visual impairment go to special schools like Linden Lodge. Others spend part or all of their school years in ordinary schools with sighted children. The important thing is that the school chosen should be the best for the child.

Many blind people, especially the newly blind, find that their greatest disability is the inability to read and write in the normal way. However, the braille system has enabled many people to overcome this handicap. Braille, devised in the early nineteenth century, can be used for all the languages, chemical symbols, shorthand, and almost everything else which can be represented by conventional printing. Blind people can use portable machines and hand instructions to make braille symbols anywhere. There are braille publishers all over the world, and blind people can obtain textbooks and other printed materials from many sources. In the UK the National Library for the Blind offers a lending service, and the RNIB offers a transcribing service as well as being a major braille printer.

For people whose sense of touch is not so good there are two alternatives: Moon type, a raised type system which is available in some English-speaking countries, and the Talking Book/Talking Newspaper schemes. Talking books and newspapers are enjoyed by great numbers of blind people whether or not they are able to read braille or Moon. The RNIB Talking Book Service is used by almost half the registered blind people in the UK.

The Royal National Institute for the Blind

The Royal National Institute for the Blind, the world's largest organisation of its kind, aims to improve the quality of life of the UK's 300,000 blind and partially sighted people.

It helps people of all ages to get good schooling, to do the same jobs as sighted people, to run their own homes, to bring up families, to enjoy sports and hobbies and to learn how to cope with losing their sight. Throughout the UK there are RNIB schools and colleges for visually handicapped children.

RNIB runs residential homes for elderly visually handicapped people, hotels, centres and services giving help with employment, rehabilitation and education.

RNIB also helps with leisure – 66,000 people all over the UK are members of the RNIB Talking Book Library. It produces vast amounts of literature in braille, Moon and on tape, and its resource centres sell over 500 subsidised items to help visually handicapped people with everyday life.

RNIB relies on donations to help it maintain and expand its services, making the difference between dependence and independence for so many blind people. Further information and literature can be obtained from:

RNIB, 224 Great Portland Street, London W1N 6AA, tel 01–388 1266.

Glossary

Antibiotic A drug which is used to kill bacteria in the body.

Braille A system for reading and writing which uses a code consisting of raised dots. Each letter of the alphabet is represented by up to six dots. There are also symbols for whole words and for groups of letters which often occur. Braille can be used for any language, for music, science and maths. Its inventor, Louis Braille, was blinded as a child.

Brailler A machine for writing braille. There are various types. The most common looks something like a typewriter but has fewer keys.

Cornea The transparent outer layer at the front of the eye. It is actually very strong but can be damaged by chemicals or by infections.

Lens A transparent object with a slightly curved surface which is used to focus rays of light. In the eye it is the lens which focuses on to the retina the light passed into the eye through the cornea.

Moon A raised type reading system for people whose sense of touch is not good.

Placenta The organ which, in a pregnant mammal, brings about the transfer of food and oxygen from mother to baby, and of waste substances from baby to mother. Other substances can also pass across the placenta.

Retina A sheet of nerve tissue, extended from the brain, at the back of the eye. In many ways it is like the film in a camera. The picture is sent to the brain via the optic nerve.

Transplant To take a living thing from one place and put it to grow somewhere else. A medical transplant means moving an organ, such as the heart, lungs or cornea, from one person's body to another's.

Index